THE VYZN PROTOCOL

CODÉ**ReVYZGen**

VYZ Interstellar

AUTHOR: Sushant Bhorge

THE VYZN PROTOCOL

Author: Sushant Bhorge

ISBN: 978-93-5627-997-1

First Edition: January 2026

Printed in India

Publisher: VYZ Interstellar > vyzinterstellar.com

WARNING

This volume contains architecture for the mind that, if integrated, may irrevocably alter the reader's perception of reality. This shift is a singular, irreversible event. By proceeding, you acknowledge this potential and assume total responsibility for the evolution of your perspective.

ॐ

तत्

to,

Motherness..

The truly high is ever low

The truly swift is ever slow

The highly sensitive is numb

The highly eloquent is dumb

The ebb and flow are but one tide

The guideless has the surest guide

The very great is very small

And he has all who gives his all

- ***Mikhail Naimy***

Abstract

From confusion to the clarity the competition co-ordinates consistently. Clarity comes with clearance of coherence. Something that cleverly collides with creativity & consumes logical conclusion not as a solution but as **the Continuum** (anant). The attempt to prove this experience as an existential truth has been done numerous times by numerous experiencers but the consistent failure generates curiosity for every newcomer.

Hence the story continues. hence me too!

I hear you.
All the time.
Say it. All that you want to say!
I'm in love with you. Badly.
So you too, Be in love.

My love.
Come.
Come. Here I am.
Im Here. Always.
All the time.
Whenever you need, whenever.
The longing to be with you.
The desire to have you embraced.
Timelessly.
Everything.

Make it happen. Come.
Come flying.
Surpass all the skies.
Now breadth for me.
Now, breadth me.

Now feel the warmth I bear.
That is solely, is yours.
Is yours,
all the time.
Let the child inside you,
play in the garden of my heart.

My love.
Didn't you realize yet the feeling I bear for you?
In life the one thing that we continuously chase.
You and me! Both.
Can't you see, it's just the love.
The love–that connects us.
The love–that reminds us of each other.
The love that kept us going
all the time.
Inspiring us to look outside and see
Something, that you share yourself with.
Solely.
im that, love. im that.

aa dubja mere samandar me
kisi lahar ki tarha
hamesha ke liye

dub meri gaharaiyon me
sama ja kisi parchai ki tarha
dono ek
hamesha ke liye

na ho fansla, mohabbat ka
na bat ho, ek hone ki
sambhal muze teri aanchal me ab
jaise ye aansma sambhale sitare ko
bezizak,
hamesha ke liye

mout rakh mere seene par ab
dhadak tu mere hi dilme
dekhe muze ab meri hi aankon se
mita de palken fir
hamesh ke liye

sun,
sama ja lihaj se
taj banu mai tera
taj bane tu mera
sama ki bache na
samane ka jariya
na koshish na halchal
samarpan na darpan
kahade tu meri
hamesha ke liye

Baby fall for me
Always.
im waiting for you.
Come. Fall. Reside.
Hide yourself within me.

In sex
be mine
totally
Do you wonder why I refuse pleasing you in intercourse?
Because in those pleasing moments I fear, you will forget me and will be with 'pleasure' instead.
No! I cant afford to do that.
I cant separate you from myself even for the sake of your pleasure.
Even your separate pleasure is my reckless rival.

Everything that falls between us is my enemy; & if the time comes, I will stand against every force that seeks to cleave us apart. I want you to become mine with such a depth that it will take infinity to find you within myself. Ultimately, looking for you within should become the play of my life. Hence melove, don't create any bond outside or I will lose you, I will lose everything.

Without you, everything is empty.

without you, what do I do!

If you are inside me, that relief will be my salvation.

That relief would be my sanctuary.

In that relief I will live my life.

Every single moment will be full of our connection.

If you are within me, knowing it in relief, I will still try to come closer.. because closeness with you has no end.

I will try to meet you again and again even if you are within me and totally mine.

How grateful it is to know that you are not outside but within!

...that I don't need to look endlessly into the eternal beyond, limitlessly into the immeasurable night!

The feeling -that whatever that I love the most, that I value the most is already resting peacefully inside me.

How grateful it is to be sure that what I want the most is not out of reach, that it is in my coverage, that I can still make a contact with it. The surety that, it is not out of reach. Somewhere, Where, I will never know, whether I will ever find it or not?

I fear you being outside me because I don't know how far this existence exists.

My love.

So, I try to take you in my arms, in my embrace. So I feel to just hide you inside me so that the darkness outside will never be able to take you away from my sight and hide you somewhere, a place, I'm unaware of. I fear I will lose you. I fear, how far, where!? Cause I don't even know how far this all is, this unreasonably vast existence. That's not even the greatest fear. The fear is, I will have to do it without you. I will have to find you without your presence, and I don't know how long it will take! What if it takes infinity and I kept on searching? Then how do I know where you are? How I know where to seek? How I know where I am? I fear, my love. So, come.

Come and reside within me.
Be mine forever.
Be mine
say it
take my name. Say it.
Let me have you forever.
if I feel, let me kiss all your body
let me have your grip
as tightly as I want
I know, you're soft,
but my desire is so strong too!
I fear, what if I break you
I fear, what if your butter like soft body failed to survive
through my disaster.

So please take this oath
take this oath
say it
say it melove

say, whatever happens,
whatever,
no matter how many times I break you, you will always survive.
And will stand through and smile. And stay ready all the time
for the next time.
Just for me.
Always.

M'love
the emptiness that I hold within me without you,
is the life that I live in your constant memory.
Will you ever come?
And satisfy?
Will you ever come and offer yourself?
forever?

The lust or desire or is it devotion, what do I name it?
Is it obsession or I call it love?
Tell me love, what I name it?
The feeling I feel for you can't be put into words because there
is no end to it.
Its illusive, its mercurial

Will you just come and handover yourself to me
and let me complete?
And then accept everything that I inflict upon you.

Accept it gracefully.
Accept it while feeling your every nerve is filled with my obsession. Be so much for me that when im gone, never knowing if I ever come back or not, still you keep on inhaling my breadth and keep on reciting my continuous memory.

Be always ready in position, such that when I come back,
I see you all up.
Ready right in position to receive me inside.
In discipline, disciplined.
Be ready all the time, don't miss a moment.
Make it your meditation.
Let the entire world meditate upon you
while you are solely concentrated on my arrival.
Let your devotion flood upon my being.
Its never about what happened to your body
that matters to me.
Our bodies just decay.
all the time!
It is never ours!

The story of your skin
is the poetry of unfolding possibilities.
Sometimes beautiful, sometimes not.

Same with your name and your lovely eyes too!
Whether I know you, whether I know your name.
whether I have seen you or not, nothing matters.
What matters is your arrival
Your sole arrival!

Your arrival, the blessing of the god.
the divine grace of his lord that made you exist,
also continues to flourish you.
What matters is you,
your existence, your soul being.
Your conscious involvement with me.
Where you constantly seek for me.
Through your thoughts, through your being,
through your emotions and through your reactions,
through your reality and grasp of ultimity,
that which is your divinity.

Be in so much love with me
be so much for me.
be there, only for me
only for me, all the time
In power, erase all distractions.
Survive through it all, to the way towards me.

Erase everything that doesn't let you concentrate.
Let your every breadth be a constant fuel
that reminds you of my existence.
Grabe me with your breadth.
Grab me tightly so that even if I lost your grip
you will still have me,
acquired.

Feel me all the time
waste no moment.
every moment should become orgasm
every moment should become a prayer
every moment should become a fight
for the survival of your focus upon my being

make it live my love
say it
say it now

pretty, say it.
even if im not there
imagine!
imagine yourself deeply filled within me.
That there is no space for you to move.
So tight in me.
Flooded.

but ..Alas
now, that I lost my love, I'm lost.
That now when I wait
I wait for the end of this constant torment.
Seamless it is.
Why don't you come and burst your flood upon this dry desert
Let the world live in their ideas, but you choose me
and make me survive.
choose me and then there should be all for me,
that which is yours.

but you said you are mine and then you were all gone.
And then I lived in misery. I told you that my life would be
incomplete and painful without you. And still knowing it all,
you left.
If you were not sure about it, why did you come?
Why did you initiate it?

Melove, Didn't I tell you that I won't be able to live through? Then why did you fail your oath? Did I even ask you to come? Didn't I tell, im good alone? That I will live my entire life in your constant memory, but if you are unsure—don't come! Even after telling this all firstly with your interests you came And then.. you left! What a joke! And then I kept on asking, why? And there was no reply, no one to reply. My mind still recites it. Still, I hear, Why? ..why! and ..why. why?

When I choose to come close, I made it all sure from my side that our relationship and my participation in relation will never break. I considered it my lifetime duty, I never looked at it like a game that many play to satisfy their urges. For me, our relationship was like a prayer to god, it was like the duty of a soldier, it was the creativity of an artist. for me, life is incomplete without the relationship that we held together. I told you this all the time, didn't you hear it? Ohh my god, that truly sucks —feels like you're dumb my love, but what to do, I chose you before knowing it. (laugh now on my fault, mortals)
Still you left, aware, that my life would be a mess, a continuous torment.
It was not more about my life alone becoming mess, but my love, why didn't you realize, it was also about the involvement of my innocent parents. Watching me in misery made them feel bad. Never you thought, watching me in pain will make my parents feel the pain too, isn't it obvious? I was afraid of this situation. And still you left and now when I see my lonely life impacting my parents, I feel it all is the result of your false labels. The lies that you fed me. I believed in them and now my entire family lives a life that they never expected. There's always a negativity that persists. It all feels negative, life feels rude, sometimes unnecessary. I feel anger, my mind body heart asks why, why and why? What was my fault? What's my parents' fault? For what we suffer? Why I can't laugh? Why my mother can't see her son living the life that every mother expects her son to live. Why I can't just smile and walk around?

Why I can't laugh anymore. At least for my mother. Why can't I lie, why can't I fake it all? Just like you.

I think of my mother. How she would have been thinking? I feel blood on mine and your hands that together we killed her son. Tell me where she will look at and feel a relief of having a son. How do I tell you that my life became a story now that I feel to avoid reading. But I walk. No! I don't expect you to come back in life and flourish it all. I continue and there is no reason in this continuation. I feel everything is pointless. Even the death, as like life feels senseless. So, I let it all happen, whatever it is. Sometimes there's intensity, sometimes theirs just numbness. Sometimes it feels like I'm the destruction of worlds and other times I become the savior.

My story is the Ramayana in which not the entire world but Sita betrayed ram. Then how this ram would win elsewhere? I see its very easy for ram to do all that, that he did because in his core of being, in his center he knew that siya is always there to fill the emptiness of his being. He knew that whether anyone else is waiting for him or not, siya is always waiting. He was sure about that one person who is missing him all the time. It inspired ram to do all that he did. It provided ram the fuel that one needs to accomplish it all. Not just inspiration and fuel but I say sita was completing ram in every moment of his being by being loyal to him. whether they were together or not —that loyalty fulfilled the lives of both Hence, no inspiration was needed, nor was any fuel needed for any karma, because the life-story itself was the love-story they were singing together. Essentially, it was never an act of indulgence or karma, but a song of the universe itself. something that we all appreciate and consider to be alike.

It was a balanced uninterrupted flow that continued naturally. But what would have happened if Siya had betrayed ram even for a second? Don't you think in ram's every moment of life, the inner emptiness would have been reflected. Let me tell you what would have happened, If Siya had betrayed ram even for a single second. (Actually, I tried to think, but I can't even think about it, so I basically asked AI to answer this question. Below, you can see the consequences that would have possibly occurred)

- *the consequences would likely have been catastrophic, though perhaps more on a spiritual and cosmic level than a literal one.*
- *Rama's entire life was defined by Dharma and his unwavering faith in Sita's purity. A moment of betrayal, even fleeting, would have fundamentally shaken his core identity and purpose.*
- *Loss of Purpose (Dharma): Rama's mission was to defeat Adharma (unrighteousness) and restore order. His belief in Sita was a pillar of his commitment to truth. A betrayal would have invalidated the entire premise of his sacrifice and struggle, making the war against Ravana feel empty.*
- *Ultimate Pain: The emotional devastation would have surpassed the pain of her kidnapping. Betrayal from the person you trust absolutely is often described as the*

most profound pain, leading to complete disillusionment.

- *and more than that, my love, The Ramayana is not just a personal story; it is a cosmic battle between good and evil. And in this situation, it would have been,*
- *Victory of Evil: If Sita's resolve, the ultimate symbol of fidelity and virtue, had fractured, it would have been seen as Adharma (unrighteousness) winning a spiritual victory over Dharma. The defeat of Ravana would have been a hollow military victory if the moral heart of the mission (Sita's purity) was already lost.*
- *The Chain of Events: The entire war, the sacrifice of Lakshmana, and the death of Ravana were all justified by the righteous cause of rescuing the pure, abducted queen. A betrayal would have dissolved this justification, turning the epic into a tragedy of flawed motives and meaningless violence.*

You see, my love, the countless deaths were justified only on the basis of Siya's purity and loyalty. Every other filthy tactic the world played and humanity experienced was justified because, simply, Siya was loyal. This is how Siya became mother to us all; her loyalty made it possible. She is valuable, not because she was a queen, but because she was a woman—a real woman: alive, aware, devoted, complete, and simply loyal.

Hence, as Ram always had Siya, even in the hardest moments—in sorrow and in pain—he survived, without any trace of loneliness or failure. Without any trace of loss. But my love, how do I live now without you? Tell me the eyes I look and reside. Tell me where I rest. Tell me who I talk to? Tell me who I complain about you and this life? Tell me what I avoid and what I accept? Should I cry or laugh on this situation? Is it worth it, or is it just worthless? Speak up my love I can't bear this silence anymore. Speak up, where are you? Did the time devour you or the darkness ate you up in this infinity.

You know what my love! Now even if the entire world came to rescue, I won't give a fuck. I don't care anyone coming anymore. It's just like a baby crying for its mother; the mother never came on time, and eventually, the child learned to live without her. Now when the mother is coming, the child feels nothing. No affection. Just like that, there was a time once I kneeled before you. I begged you to stop. Something that I never thought I will ever have to do in life. You made it all happen and yet you never listened. It was terrifying to see a life without you so I did everything I was capable of. I tried every tactic and the more I tried the more I realized that you never understood me, the more I realized that your words were merely sweet lies with no meaning and life in it. The more I tried the more I realized that, how heartless this existence could be. The more I tried the more you showcased how determined you were to not listen to me and stand by your side to showcase how much right you are about your decisions. But my love, where this determined person was when you were promising me a relationship forever? My love why didn't you just kill my every nerve before introducing me this reality; full of lies and deception.

Now its such that I'm so much in continuation in this loneliness that I find it normal. I know, I feel its painful, but that's my natural being now. I accepted it gracefully cause that's your gift. Filthy it is, but yours! So, there is no struggle for anything. Whatever comes, I just don't care. I know there is nothing more to lose, because I already lost it all by losing you. My love.

Baki ye duniwale to duniyawale hai. Marne ke bad bohot kimat hogi in labjo ki unki najar me. Blickul Van gogh ke paintings ki tarah. Ye duniyawale dekhtehe duniyawalon ke najar se, inki khudki koi aankh nhi najar nhi ya samaz nhi. Bheed inko chalati hai, wo bheed ko chalate hai. Ye dar me, milke sath chalate hai. Thik bhi hai kyonki, bheed me aantrik dar se mukti mil jati hai, kyonki bheed ki apani taqad hoti hai, jo anekon se ek hoti hai. Inhe mari kahaniya pasand hai. Ek jiti jagati kahani se vo darate hai kyonki ek jinda kahani me inhe badalaw ka khatara mehsus hota hai. Jis kahani ke kirdar khatam hue wo kahani unke liye jinda ho jati hai. Yahi is gulamon se bhari duniya ka vusul hai. Unke bich bhi koi sochanewala jarur hoga jo gulamon se khudko khada karke apne badshah hone ki gazal auron ko sunayega. Yahi to ham hai. Yahi to hai meri jamat. Jamin se uthakar khada hoke hum gana gate hai. Hamare jindadili ka, baikhouf. tum jaise murdon ke bich, mankar ki kabhi na kabhi ye murde bhi jinda honge aur jan payenge wo jo ye abhitak samaz hi na paye.
par shayad, tere nasamzi ki koi had nahi!

My love, how do I tell you. My love. Something meant a lot. Something meant more than life, more than anything that was known. It was simply beyond words so im very sorry even though I tried I failed to word it. But didn't you see it in my eyes? How do I tell you now that my morning starts with reminding me the entire story of our relationship. Every morning, the first moment in morning makes me aware of your absence. It tells me that I already lost it all in the very first moment of the day where many beings usually start some sort of struggle to get better in their life, I see it all already a failure. I feel numb. I see I'm lost. What I can win in this existence and tell myself that I have got something after losing you in the first place, love. And you know what, before we got into relationship, when it was all one-side, when I was aware of your desire for me and yet we were not together. In those fulfilling moments, I felt I was winning everything, because I saw you not separated from me. Even though we were not together, the feeling, the knowing that I feel something for you and you too feel the want to be with me was enough for me to live every day with great happiness. Yes. There was relief. And then when you were coming in my life I told you if we got into relationship and by chance, if I lost you — I won't be able to bear it all and live the same. Even after warning innumerous times, you came and then left. Wow! Why don't I call you cruel? What do I conclude out of it? Do I laugh on myself that the person I considered the most and the person who told me that —im so valuable to her, was just having some fun with me and never truly realized the depth of our conversation. Who do I complain all this? If I never accepted anyone else's authority other than yours. Mortals! Tell me, how do I approach my accused and ask for justice? Do i ask for taking a judgment? Or do I just make a decision and punish the one who is in charge of the sins? Or do I let the god decide it all? But who the fuck is the god? What is god? If this god named entity created this mess and is responsible for this, I would love to have a meeting with him/it and grab his caller and ask why in the first place, 'you gave me this life without fucking asking me?' well I don't think I will do this, cause see, if he/she/it (god) is greatest as it is considered by people, personally, god should not in the first place intervene in anything that is going on in here. If god is manipulating or any other entity is controlling this continuum, it all becomes pointless and I'm not even interested in knowing about these different levels because all that I care about is now, and now I feel, I'm lost without you, so I ask for justice, but who do I ask? Do I ask to government? But they will ask if I started it all by creating any bond, document, stamp paper or written papers with signature of both? They do not accept and consider the relief I felt in those pleasing moments. The relief of having you once and forever, the trust that you will stay forever, no matter what, the feeling that I got it all by having you and then feeling inspired and ready for anything that life throws at me. But. I lost it all. How do I explain this to the government and court because what they consider 'truth' is -papers. And I don't have papers. Obviously, the thought never came in my mind. I never felt the eyes like yours, can lie so severely. Who knew you were the master of a game that I have no idea about, hence I never *understood the game you were playing with me until I found myself far away from your territory where truthfulness exists, of course without you and then I got to know the truth that you are never with me! How crazy and unjustly it is to think and accept it all so obviously. Itz _**H**ARD. Once, I though your oath was as lovely, innocent and transparent as like your eyes but you proved I'm a daydreamer. Then will I ever get justice? Now tell me who I ask it for? Is there any end to it? Which endless loop you put me inside, melove.*

Ye sab hokar bhi agar tu muze puchata hai ki kya hai mere pas. Kya hai meri aukat jo tu ruke mere pas? Jab mein puchta hu ye sawal khudse to aawaz aati hai,

gava diya tune jo tha tere pas
ab kya puch rha hai kya hai mere pas

jab bahar tha tab tu roya
baharon ki khushi me
aaj bhi tu ro hi rha
khud ke is khudkhushi me

ye manjar dekh tuze hansi nhi aati
mere barish ke mausam me bhi
ab barish barish nahi lati

kyona basa leta ab tu shahar ek apana
jahan bs ronewale gujare, ronewalon ki basti se
dhunde sabhi eksath, wo jo sabne khoya hai
jashna manaye sabhi, mohabbat ke matam ka
chillaye sabhi roye, gaye apanehi dhun me
kahaniya dohrayen sabhi bar bar
Mohabbat ke apani,
Qayamat me apne

mere mehboob,
bata,
ab me kis najar teri taraf dekhu
tune to meri hi virasat me muze hi dastan bana diya!

ab chalta hu mein
to parchai najar aati hai.
us parchai me muze,
bss tu najar aati hai.

samzata hu jahan me sab
khuda ka kiya karaya hai
par ye mera junun hi hai
jo tuze khuda karar deta hai

mana ki harkar jita hu me, fir bhi
mere jamat ki kaum, me badhana nahi chahta,
koshish se milegi muze, teresath har ek cheez
par zamane se rutha me ab, kuch kamana nhi chahta.
chahata hu rat
jo mita de hamesha ke liye
chahtahu aag
jo jalade hamesha ke liye
chahta hu jism tera
jo chinke mere dard pe
chahtahun ek jahan
barakarar hamare hone se
jahan aankhe do
aur najar ek ho
tera mera hona
*_**H**AKK, beshak ho.*

Jahan gau me
to mehfil teri
chahun me to saajish teri
agar chand nikle
to nikale hamare liye
barish bhi aaye
to ruke hamare liye
gaye mausam
geet hamare bahar ka
sajaye khuda
rahen tere mere liye

mange ful
rounak tere mere liye
ruke maut
tere mere liye
bole maut
shayad me bhi zinda hoti
to dhadkan banati, hamesh ke liye,
sirf,
tere aur mere liye.

Sirf tere- mere liye
ye geet ye bahar
ye rounak ye jashna
kya inme bhi koi sachhai hai?
Tere jism aur ruh ki chahat me
meri khudsehi ek ladai hai

teri jan lu
ya meri ruh dedu
rakhu khudko tere pas
ya banalun apna tuze
ya mitadu ye fansala
ham dono ko mitakar
ya apnalu tuzko
apni is ruh me
dhakakar tuzko
mere is jism se

Shhh...Bol mat.
bas dekh meri najar me
bhul najar ko apne
is najar ko dekhte dekhte

kalam syahi mitakar likh tu
nam apana har mohabbat ki kahani me
bhulkar bhi jamana mita na paye
kahani apni, jahan ke panno se

kaun kahata hai
mohabbat har wakt jawan nhi hoti
puch mere dilko, dhadkata hai abhabhi tere liye
mere kahani me har wakt
ful khilta hai tere liye
jamana jita hai tereliye
aansama chat tereliye
jamin takk tereliye

tereliye khuda
tereliye khuda ka aana
tereliye khuda ka bahana
tereliye khuda ki dawat
tereliye khuda ki mehfil
mehfil me hui meri maut
meri maut se meri ma ka rona
uske rone par bhi tera na aana
fir khudko meri yunhi dulhan batana

mehfil me fir tera bar bar aana
aakar janaje pe aansu bahana
wo aansu nahi qatl hai mere dil ka
kyonki saajish teri thi, fasane ki muzko
wo jo saajish teri thi jalane ki dilko
wo saajish meri ja, bohot rang lai
hoti hai roj roj jo gharame ladhai
kahate hai log pagal aashik aawara
roya mein jaise, teri harkat se mara

mere junun ki saja tune muze to dedi
apne junun ko todkar, jamane ke liye
par ab insaf ka bhukha
insan mere bhitar ka
puch raha hai mere maut ki wajah
puch rah hai, thi wo galti kiski
jo mere ma ko uska beta gavana pada

jane de, chod de wo sab
usase tera kya jata hai!
tere ma ko to tu aise hi salamat hai
ghar sansar to jal raha hai mera, tere jahan to waise hi khushamat hai

meri ja
ye jahan shayad bohot bada hai
shayad yaha khoi hui chize milti hi nhi
shayad yaha jo bichad jata hai
bas bichad jata hai ek anjane safar me
khoji dhundata rah jata aakhari sans tak
bas ek yad ke silsile ke saye me
wo roushani bhi nasib nhi na saya karib se
ki musafir peecha kare us roushani ka
aur thake to gale lagaye usi roshani ko

shayad tere sajish ka dour hi
mere jindagi ka sukun tha
teri sajish jo safal hui
katara katara jahan ka
mil gaya tuze aakar
hava ka rukh dekhte dekhte

tabse ab kya batau meri ja
bohot sambal sambal kar jeeta hu
girne ka dar nhi hai muzko
fir khada hone se darta hu

dikhta hai samzata hu
mere safar ka hoi hal nhi
mere manzil ka koi kal nhi
mere koshish ka koi fal nhi
aur meri ja..
mere kwahish ka koi pal nhi.

Muze milega ya nhi
ye bhi ab sawal nhi
tere mere karib jane ka
ab koi khayal nhi

subah milti hai sham milti hai
terebina ab ye sans bhi chalti hai
aahat bhi hoti hai, pata bhi chalta hia
terebina meri ja, ye suraj bhi dhalta hia

bas kami hai to hai tere us zuth ki
jisko ye pagal insan, sach samaz baitha tha
zamane se ladkar wo, teri tarf chalta tha

jita tha tuze
manta tha tuze
subah se rat tak
gata that tuze
bas janata tha wo tuze
chalta tha tere rah par

shayad meri ja
use, gharme basana tha tere
dhundhakr tuze, tuzme khona tha use
lekin jankar sacchai
tut gaya sitara tukdon me

us sitare ki kahani
sitara hi jiya hai
dekh-sun kar tum
kya use samaz paoge
jo usane jiya tha
jo usne socha tha
uske wo pal
kaise tum jan paoge?
Aur fir wo bhulega bhi kaise?
Wo sab, jo uski duniya ban chuka tha
mana ki wo duniya tut gayi
par yadon, khayalon me
ab bhi kuch zinda hai
jo dohrata hai
usi kahani ko bar bar
lagan se aaghosh me
jaise ki wo silsila
ek gahana ban gaya ho!

kaise samzau meri ja
yad karta hu tuze, har wakt
wo zindagi ban chuki hai ab
jaise ki ek dhyan
ek aisi darar jisase mera koi fansala nhi

han, zaroor!
Ab waqif hu tuzse
teri acchai aur buraiyon se
fir bhi apanaya hai tuze
teri gaharayiyon ko jankar

jana hai tuzme
hai meri nafarat
Mohabbat tu meri
Hai tu hi Qayamat

To fir meri jana
Kyon hai ye duri?
Kyon hai andhera?
Fir kyon savera?

Kyon hai ye halchal
Mohabbat me tere
Hai kis ki ye sajish
Jataneki isko

Rulati hai sajish
Hasati hai halchal
Darati hai palpal
Magan se magan me

to Dekhu kaha mai
Jo rag-rag se waqeef
Sochu tuze mei
To halchal se waqeef

To bata meri jana
ki jana kaha hai?
Ki tu meri manzil
Ya mai teri manzil?

Shayad kisine
Ye socha na hoga
Kaha tu kaha mai
Ye Milana na hoga

Magar fir bhi jana
Jo hota hai dil se
Wo hone laga hai
Magan se magan mai

Chahat ki dekho
Ho duri bana lu
To lagata hai palpal
Hun zinda ya murda

Magar fir bhi jana
Ki zinda hu harpal
Qayamat me teri
Mohabbat me teri

Abhi kya abhi to
Hai chalna hai tabtaq
Jahan taq hai chalna
Waha taq hai chalna

Chalne mai humdum
Yaden teri hai
Sayen me harpal
Zalake teri hai
Teri hai ye palake
Jo tuzko hi dhundhe
Teri hi rahon mein
Akele akele.

meri ja, ab tu
baton ke par jana
kahana nhi kuch
bas aake gale lagana

mafi ke to tu layak hi nhi
bas aake thahar jana mere pas
pighalke muzme aawaz ban jana

wahi aawaj jo gunjati hai muzme
wahi aawaz jo gati hai muzko
wahi aawajjo chalati hai muzko

meri ja
bas karib aa jana utane
ke kahana pau me aawaz koi aur
dekh na pau koi nazara kisi aur
bas tuhi bane zindagani meri ja
zeeu bas tuze me, andar, bahar, charo aur

(I was hesitant to include this, but it emerged as the perfect reflection of an indefinite state that continues. So, get ready for it.)

communism, rashtravadi, samosa, kachouri
sab bhul jau tere sayen me chori
sant mahatma ye guru waigere
bhad me jaye sab sanz savere
ye aakad ki dadi hamesha ka mama
mitade tu muzse, ye nachiz panama

bakwas ye dil ka
nikale tu muzse
basale tu khudko
ab dhadkan me meri

pata hai ki nhi hai tu kisi aur
jatata hu boton me sapanon ko tere
mitata hu chahat, palon ka tadpana
nasha hai ye mera, ye likhna likhana
bhulatahu duri fansala do jaha ka
smzata hu ek din wo smzegi chahat

ab chahta na me
koi aur manzil
is manzil ne beshak
nakare hai ye dil

ye dil
ye dil jo beshak
hai chahat ke mare
ye andhe hai beshak
ye sare ke sare

tu aana
tu aake
tu inko, jalana
jalake, meri ja
inhe fir fasana
fasake ke tu inme
fir chahat jagana
ye andhe ke andhe
fir thaharenge ek din
ki payenge khudko
na thahra na zinda
banake tu qutil
sabhi ki meri ja
badshahon me apani
jagah ek banana

tere aashiq to murda
tuhi ek jo zinda
to khudko tu apni
jahan mai sajana

tere us jaha ke
tere us mahal mai
numaish tu karana
mere is jisam ki

ki kahana sabhi ko
ye jeeta hai tune
tere ek safar me
hazaron safar ke

tu mahir hai usme
tu malik usi ka
ustad jo thahara
tu aaka safar ka

Riyaz mai tera
Hu panchi ek subah ka
Teri subah na ek hai
Na shame anokhi

Zamane ki shame
Hai tere hi jaisi
Panchi hazaron
Na **ek** *unme shamil*

Fir,
zamane se rutha
anutha parinda
parinda jo nikla
ye ghayal parinda
jamane ne isko
sajake sawara
inhone isiko

he apna banaya
apna banake
ise fir nachaya
jamane ki mehfil
me ghayal parinda
tadpe ki roye
ki nache ki gaye
inhe kya, inhe to
hai mehfil sazana
zamane ki mehfil
zamana hi jane
parinde ko inse
khata ab na hoga

dekho dekho,
ab to maut ki rah dekhte dekhte
parinda thahar chuka hai
inke zulm aur nainsafi ka
ab hal nikal chuka hai

meri ma muze tu
ab wapis bulade
na jaunga fir kab
is jamane me zuthe
ye zamana hai khuni
hai matlab ka mara

inhe na pata hai
chahat ki halchal
halchal to inko
hai khatre ki ghanti

sajaya to tera
kamayan to mera
paraya na apna
hai apna karibi
karibi me halchal
na inko pasanda hai
hai darte hai sabse
ye darna hai halchal

hame to meri ma
na saajish pata thi
pata thi na muzko
ye duniya ki halchal
sikhayi na tune
ye riten jaha ki
ki hara tabhi me
saajish me uske

wo boli
meri ja
me rah lungi har din
wo boli ki hardam
me hun tuzme shamil
wo kahati thi dinme
sitare hai mere
raton me chanda
mein suraj usika

wo kahati thi harpal
meri ja meri ja
jamane me bas tu
muze ek kaabil

na lagati thi muzko
wo bate aawara
kahta tha me bhi
hu tera me tera

samaza ki hu me
zamane me sacche
baten jo uski thi
lankhon ke parche

bahon me uski
tha rab maine paya
aankhen wo uski
khudaya khudaya

teri yad aati thi bahon me uske
baton me milti thi teri hi zalke
bani thi wo shohrat
bani thi wo doulat
zamane ki ranjish me
pyari si mohlat

meri ma ab tu bhi sochti hogi ki wo thi bhi to kitni pyari thi?
that you might have been wondering how someone could be
that kind of pretty! Right!?
So let me tell you mother, how pretty she was!

wo itani thi pyari
ki suraj saja de
sawaren jo khudko
to barish gira de

wo barish me pani
wo pani me halchal
wo halchal khudaki
wo badhati hi jaye

oh si Suraj subah da
oh si chand vi tārē,
oh si sukh dē savere
oh si sukh dē nazare

mere nal si tasali
thi sajada khuda ka
thi kya thi wo muzko
khuda mera jane!

wo payi jo manzeel
mili na jo kwahish
wo pane ki khwahish
wo jeene ki manzeel!

wo jeena hai mushkeel
hai rone ki noubat
re bhago wahase
jo bhage salamat

jo atake
wo bhatke
unhe ab na rahat
mehfil sajado
hason tum usipe

wo hara wo ataka
wo bhataka, khudise
jo fisla wahi pe
wo hara khudise

sabhi tum milon aaj
mehfil sajado
hason tum usipe.
Ki dekho wo hara

jo jeeta tha harpal
wo apanon se hara
jo bahata tha harpal
ab khudmehi thahara

ye chikhe usi ki
ye aandhi adhuri
na chinkhe hai tadpan
jara tum bhi jano

ye tadpan jo mehsus hoti hai dilme
wo tadpan teri hai, meri sirf gatha

ye gatha dikhati hai tuzako jo tera
ye gatha hai darpan, twa-gatha sa-gatha

pahachan dekha, wo tune tuziko
jo dekhe to lagata hai aadha adhura

tu gata hai isko, ye teri hai gatha
ye tera hai gana ye tera sunana

ye aawaj teri, jo sunta hai harpal
ye rachana hai teri, tu fasata hai harpal

ye dhundha hai tune jo khudko tu paya
ye koshish tumhi ho tumhi ne rachaya

jo dekhen kisi aur, manjar tumhi ho
Safar ye tumhi ho, safina tumhi ho
Mohabbat mai aashiq-hasina tumhi ho
jano to makka-madina tumhi ho

tumhi ho wo karta
jo karana hi jane
tumhi ho wo gyata
jo jane na jane
ye rachana adhuri
hai puri adhuri
ye jane to samze
na jane to soche
hai soche adhuri
adhure me
pure ko
dekhe to

jano ki
pura hai
saccha hai
kaccha hai
baccha hai
hoga wo
ek din jo
har pal me
pura tha
chalne me saya tha
koshish me paya tha
mehfil me gaya tha
ranjish me chaya tha
sawalon me aaya tha
gujarish bhi thi uski
par har wakt—gawaya tha.
use to,
rato ne laya tha
din me sajaya tha
dosti aur chahat ko
usi ne chalaya tha
wo tha,
aate aate yuhi aaneme
aur aakar tum me mil janeme
jo mila abhi abhi
wo tumse hokar gujarata tha
jo pakda tumne abhi abhi
wo tumko fir jakhdta tha

ye silsila fir jari tha
silsile me wo jari tha
jananewale par gaye
silsila tab bhi jari tha

wo bahta tha bahata tha
usime sub samata tha

wo ful tha tuzise khila
wo mehak thi har jagah teri

us mehek ko tuhi dhundhta tha
dhundhne me aate jate
tuhi tuzko milta tha

tha wo har jagah se
pukarata har dam
har pukar me khudki
puchta tha wo khudse
atak atak ke puche
ye puchna ye kya hai?
Jo puchne me ataka
wo sawalon me latake
latake so bhatake
bhatakta hi jaye

suno tum kahani
magan se tumhari
magan me khilegi
bagawat wo nyari
wo bagawat na teri
khuda usme chamke
he kanfi wo zalke
jo tuzko jala de

ye kahana hai koshish
ye likhana hai koshish
ye koshish teri hai
ye koshish hai barkat
koshish me tere
hai ek anityadhara
jo jode sabhi ko
tuze aur muze bhi
yahi se to aati hai
jannat ki khwahish
yahi se to milti hai
mausam ko barish
yahi hai khudaya
khudayat ka bahana
yahi hai khudaya
khudayat ki mehfil

bohot khub!

To aakhirkar is mukam tak hum pohoch hi gaye jaha khuda ki mulaqat khud se hone lagati hai, bus khuda hi bolta hai aur khuda hi sunta hai. Magan khudme.

Yog.

C-O-N-C-L-U-S-I-O-N

The VYZN Protocol is an expression of continuity translated into poetic format to define the creative roadmap of human emotional intelligence which inspires beings to maintain a collective connection in a naturally evolved organization which otherwise known to us as—Society.

This rooted connection is felt with immense depth by almost all aware beings but at the same time, an environment full of ignorance can eliminate the intensity as well the ability to feel it and in such environment the definition of values changes as per the direction of collective conscious flow. The purpose of this book is to enlighten readers to this collective natural habit and introduce you all to an interactive platform where creation, choice, and consciousness play together to make player aware of the philosophy that creates us and defines our being.

To particularly begin with this, I dedicate this book to the gaming project of VYZ Interstellar – ReVYZGen (Result VYZVERSE Genesis).

To proceed with this, I invite all the readers who read and found the book interesting to reach out and share your ideas to define the game world. As always--your creativity will never be bordered. You know what that mean! Right? so come up with anything and together we will convert your ideas into a form that reflects you. Again, thank you for sharing time together on this lovely planet earth. Unleash your creativity and let's build the VYZ together. Limitlessly!

To lock in,

Visit: www.vyzinterstellar.com

Email: team@vyzinterstellar.com

Stay Creative,

SUSHANT BHORGE

Founder, VYZ Interstellar

www.ingramcontent.com/pod-product-compliance
Lightning Source LLC
Chambersburg PA
CBHW062202160726
48282CB00027B/965
9789356279971